MADE IN BRITAIN

How the UK Makes Torture and Death its Business

Amnesty International United Kingdom
London

ISBN 1873328214

First published February 1997
Amnesty International United Kingdom
99—119 Rosebery Avenue,
London EC1R 4RE

This report was written and researched by the Military, Security and
Police Transfers Group of Amnesty International United Kingdom

Designed by The Harrington Consultancy
Printed by Ennisfield Print and Design.

CONTENTS

INTRODUCTION

A prison block in Saudi Arabia, a police cell in China, an execution ground in the United Arab Emirates, a protest demonstration in Zimbabwe... all may seem far removed from the United Kingdom, but all have one thing in common: the 'Made in Britain' label. All are places where security equipment from the UK has been used to commit human rights violations.

Amnesty International works worldwide for the release of prisoners of conscience, fair trials for political prisoners and an end to torture, extrajudicial executions, 'disappearances' and the death penalty. Its 1996 Annual Report documented human rights violations and abuses in 147 countries in the world. Foreign equipment and training is often used by military, security and police forces, and by opposition groups, in committing such violations and abuses. One of the ways in which Amnesty International works to prevent human rights violations is by seeking to stop the supply of such equipment and training, and by calling on governments to implement sufficient safeguards in their export policies.

Amnesty International campaigns against the transfer of military, security and police equipment, personnel or training, as well as direct practical or financial support for such transfers, that can reasonably be assumed to contribute to human rights abuses in the receiving country. The UK is a major exporter of training, equipment and personnel to security forces overseas, and makes some provision for control and prevention of exports of such equipment under the regularly updated Export of Goods (Control) Order (EG(C)O). However, this book documents cases which demonstrate how the EG(C)O can be evaded; how the secrecy surrounding the trade prevents proper monitoring by Parliament and by non-governmental organisations like Amnesty International; and how the UK's export regulations, as currently implemented, fail to prevent the UK from contributing to human rights violations elsewhere in the world.

Suggestions for further reading on specific countries or issues are contained in Appendix III.

1 BENDING THE RULES

Evading controls on military, security and police transfers

'Any application for the export of leg-irons would be refused'
Michael Heseltine, President of the Board of Trade, letter to Michael Howard MP, 1 March 1995

In 1993, a British businessman called Patrick Foster was imprisoned in Saudi Arabia for drinking alcohol, which is prohibited there. He was chained and shackled in leg-irons. He smuggled a diary out of the prison in cigarette packets. It was somewhat ironic, he wrote, that 'the shackles and cuffs in this establishment are made by Hiatts in England'. Patrick Foster's story, told in a Channel 4 television documentary *Dispatches* (first shown on 11 January 1995), is just the latest chapter in the long history of Hiatts' involvement in this trade.

The Birmingham company was first discovered exporting leg-irons from the UK in 1983. Two reporters from the *Daily Mirror* posed as potential buyers of Hiatts' products, and were offered supplies of leg-irons, gang-chains and other restraining equipment. Their article stated that Hiatts claimed to have been making leg-irons for over 200 years, since the time of the slave trade.

Leg-irons are designed to severely restrict a prisoner's movement. They make the wearer unstable and liable to overbalance, and can cause chafing of skin. Welts and sores will appear after approximately 24 hours. During a visit to Pakistan in November 1994, an Amnesty International delegation saw several prisoners whose ankles were bandaged because they had become sore from the iron fetters rubbing against them; on top of the bandages the prisoners still wore shackles and iron bars.

Leg-irons can also be used to facilitate torture. Patrick Foster witnessed this in Saudi Arabia: he saw prisoners hung upside down by the leg-irons they were wearing. Sipho Pityana, a former prisoner in South Africa, described on a BBC *Watchdog* programme in 1984 how leg-irons were used to torture him: 'They tied electric wires on the irons.... so the iron was a contact between the flesh and the electric device'. Sipho also described how his captors used the leg-irons to hold him in the sea upside down, under water, for what seemed to him to be endless periods of time. The use of leg-irons is prohibited under Rule 33 of the United Nations' Standard Minimum Rules for the Treatment of Prisoners which states that: 'Instruments of restraint, such as handcuffs, chains, irons and strait-jackets, shall never be applied as punishment. Furthermore, chains or irons shall not be used as restraints'. Amnesty International opposes the export and manufacture of military, security or police equipment such as leg-irons and believes that using them on prisoners is a form of cruel, inhuman or degrading treatment.

Following the 1983 *Daily Mirror* article exposing Hiatts, a number of concerned MPs joined Amnesty International's campaign to have the trade stopped. Their efforts were met initially with a lamentable response. As questions were raised in Parliament about the export of leg-irons, Norman Tebbit, then Secretary of State for Trade and Industry replied that: '.... if this country didn't export them, someone else would' (*Hansard*, 14 December 1983). Amnesty International believes that our Government has a moral and political duty to do everything possible to prevent the abuse of human rights; this includes preventing UK companies from contributing to human rights violations by trading in military, security and police equipment which can be used for torture. In the words of Pierre Sane, Amnesty International's Secretary General: 'this is money which is earned on the blood of victims' (Channel 4 *Dispatches* documentary *Back on the Torture Trail*, March 1996).

Only after intensive lobbying by MPs and campaigning by Amnesty International did the Government agree to include leg-irons, shackles and gang-chains in its export controls. In March 1984, Mr Tebbit assured the House of Commons that:

> 'Licences will not be issued for the export to any destination of leg-irons, shackles and gang-chains for the restraint of prisoners. Applications for export licences for other purposes – for example, for theatrical performances or museum display – will be considered on their merits'.
>
> (*Hansard*, 28 March 1994).

11

In 1991, two human rights researchers attending an exhibition of security equipment in Miami called COPEX (the Covert and Operational Procurement Exhibition) were given a brochure advertising 'leg cuffs'. Although the address given in the brochure was that of a US registered company, Hiatt Thompson, the brochure indicated that the equipment was manufactured in Birmingham, England, and was distributed on a stall registered in the name of *Hiatt and Company Ltd* of Birmingham.

Amnesty International alerted its members about the overseas promotion of leg cuffs and, following questions raised by MPs, Tim Sainsbury, then Minister of State for Trade and Industry, launched an official inquiry into the trade.

On 17 October 1991, Mr Sainsbury announced – 'in the light of publicity' – that 'oversized cuffs' and certain linking chains, which could be used for the same purpose as leg-irons, had been evading UK export controls. He included oversized cuffs in the existing export ban on leg-irons, shackles and gang-chains. The maximum length permitted for two cuffs and a linking chain is now 240mm. 'I have sought advice from the police scientific development branch of the Home Department about the definition of *handcuff*', said Mr Sainsbury.

In 1992, Amnesty International reported that Orton Chirwa, a 72 year-old prisoner of conscience in Malawi, had been held in British-made leg-irons. He was handcuffed, leg-ironed and held in a squatting position by a metal bar behind his knees for two days and nights. According to a report of the case in *The Guardian*, the chairman of Hiatts, Geoffrey Cross, acknowledged that leg-irons used in Malawi prisons were probably provided by his company. But he said that Hiatts had not manufactured or sold leg-irons since their export from the UK was banned in 1984.

In January 1995 Channel 4's *Dispatches* documentary 'The Torture Trail' took Patrick Foster, the man who was imprisoned in Saudi Arabia, to visit Hiatts' offices in Birmingham, to confront Hiatts about the leg-irons he had seen. The director they spoke to said:

> 'We've stopped making leg cuffs and those were dispatched as hand cuffs.... I don't have to dictate or tell anybody what to do with the tools they get. That's not my problem, they do exactly as they like.'

The Channel 4 team were able to buy Hiatts' leg cuffs in the USA. It would seem that Hiatts had been exporting oversized handcuffs to the USA, where Hiatt Thompson add longer chains to turn them into leg cuffs, whose sale and export is still legal in the USA. In response to Amnesty International members' letters to their MPs following the *Dispatches* television programme, Michael Heseltine replied for the Department of Trade and Industry: 'Any application for the export of leg-irons would be refused'. But the Hiatts story shows just how easily the UK's export controls can be evaded. Amnesty International is calling for these regulations to be changed to safeguard human rights.

BOARD of DIRECTORS

P. Atkins

2 PUTTING HUMAN RIGHTS FIRST

Considering human rights criteria in export controls

*'We look carefully at applications for [export] licences ....
paying particular attention to the human rights record of the
country concerned'*
David Davis, Minister of State for Foreign and Commonwealth Affairs,
letter to Keith Mans MP, 7 April 1995

UK controls on military, security and police transfers

The Export of Goods (Control) Order is the principle regulation in
the UK which controls the export of arms, military and security
equipment. It was established under the Import, Export and
Customs Powers (Defence) Act (1939) and is updated every few
years, most recently in 1994. Under the terms of this order, the
export of certain goods is prohibited without a licence, and a
company wishing to export goods which fall under its remit must
apply to the Export Control Organisation at the Department of
Trade and Industry (DTI), giving details of the product, its
destination and who the end user will be. In deciding whether to
approve a licence application, the DTI consults with the Foreign
Office to ascertain the foreign policy implications of the sale, and
with the Ministry of Defence for the strategic and security aspects
of the sale. Licences are then issued, or applications refused, in
accordance with the advice received from these two Government
departments. A set of guidance notes for Foreign and
Commonwealth Office desk officers clearly states Government
policy: 'to encourage the sale of UK defence equipment unless
there are compelling reasons for not doing so'. Amnesty
International believes that the violation of human rights constitutes
one such compelling reason.

The Foreign and Commonwealth Office has responsibility for
considering the implications for human rights of a proposed export
of military equipment. Amnesty International has continually asked
the UK Government for more information on how a country's

14

human rights record would affect the export of military, security and police equipment to that country. The Government's reply is always that the behaviour of the recipient country and its human rights record are considered before an export licence is granted. No details of this procedure are given. There is therefore no public scrutiny of the information used in considering a country's human rights record when applications to export equipment under the Export of Goods (Control) Order are examined. For example, when Ann Clwyd MP asked for details of the criteria used when deciding not to export arms to countries which abuse human rights, the reply from David Davis (Minister of State at the Foreign and Commonwealth Office) was simply that:

> 'applications for export licences for defence equipment are considered case by case on the basis of agreed criteria which include the internal situation in the country of final destination.'
> (*Hansard*, 27 March 1995).

The Official Secrets Act of 1911 prevents disclosure of any information likely to affect the UK's security, no matter how minor. This means that the Government has no obligation to disclose details of arms exports. But the disclosure of criteria upon which its decisions about exports are based would surely not affect security. Amnesty International aims to ensure that the human rights situation in receiving countries *is* systematically taken into consideration before decisions are made about transfers of military, security and police equipment or training. Such transfers should not take place unless it can be demonstrated that they will not contribute to human rights violations. UK export controls do not meet this requirement – despite assurances that human rights criteria are always considered no details about these criteria have been disclosed.

Sale of arms to Nigeria
The Government has allowed military and security equipment sales to Nigeria and other countries such as Indonesia and Turkey with records of persistent human rights violations. In doing so, the Government has failed to give more than simple assurances that equipment will not be used for internal repression. The detailed

assessments or procedures which give rise to such assurances have not been revealed.

In Nigeria, human rights violations have escalated in recent years. Although political opposition is not formally prohibited, critics of the government are still harassed and detained, and there have been reports of torture, ill-treatment and extrajudicial killings by the security forces, as well as mass public executions and the detention – often without trial – of numerous prisoners of conscience. The UK has been one of the largest exporters of arms and security equipment to Nigeria.

Nigeria's security forces include the 'Internal Security Task Force', reported to have carried out at least 50 political killings in 1994 in Ogoniland, where local people are waging a campaign against the environmental damage brought about by the oil industry. The Internal Security Task Force is a paramilitary force which includes the Mobile Police, who travel in armoured vehicles and are always armed. They are known locally as 'Kill'n'Go'. At least some of the vehicles they use have been supplied by a UK firm, GKN Defence Ltd, which has numbered the Nigerian Mobile Police among customers for export of its Saxon 4 x 4 Armoured Personnel Carrier. The Saxon is suitable for a wide range of internal security roles.

In December 1993, following the annulment of Nigeria's elections, the UK and its European Union (EU) partners announced measures to restrict arms sales to Nigeria. In the UK, this meant that all new applications for export licences for defence and security equipment to Nigeria would be examined on a case-by-case basis, with the 'presumption of denial'. In June 1995, however, it was revealed that the UK Department of Trade and Industry had granted at least 30 licences for the sale of defence equipment to the Nigerian police and army, including firearms, rubber bullets, CS gas, spare parts for weapons and military vehicles. Furthermore, Baroness Chalker, Minister of State at the Foreign and Commonwealth Office, claimed that the EU embargo did not apply to weapons sales 'where military equipment is to be used by the police, or forces taking part in international peacekeeping operations'.

In November 1995, following the execution of Ken Saro-Wiwa and eight other Ogoni campaigners, the UK Government and its 14

EU partners announced that restrictions on arms sales to Nigeria would be extended. However, it was still not made clear whether this embargo would cover 'non-lethal' paramilitary, riot control and police equipment, all of which could directly contribute to human rights violations.

While Amnesty International neither supports nor opposes arms embargoes, the gross human rights violations carried out by the Nigerian security forces have led Amnesty International to question the continued supply of paramilitary and riot control police equipment and of spare parts for previously supplied military vehicles.

Sale of armoured vehicles to Indonesia

On 2 March 1995 Michael Heseltine, then President of the Board of Trade, announced to the House of Commons that he had authorised a licence to Alvis Vehicles for the export of armoured vehicles to Indonesia. He stated that:

> 'The decision has been made in the light of the established and internationally agreed criteria for military exports. It has included a thorough assessment of the likelihood of these vehicles being used for internal repression in Indonesia or East Timor. This assessment has concluded that it is not likely that these vehicles would be so used.'

Indonesia's rulers came to power after the 1965 coup and in the aftermath of one of the worst massacres in recent history. In less than a year up to one million people were killed and at least as many imprisoned. In December 1975 Indonesian forces invaded East Timor, and the massive military presence in the territory since then has meant two decades of terror for its people. As many as 270 people are believed to have died in the massacre of peaceful demonstrators which took place at the Santa Cruz cemetery in Dili in 1991. One eye-witness testified that some of the wounded taken to the military hospital in Dili were crushed by military vehicles as they lay on the ground. Systematic human rights violations are a continuing feature of Indonesia's illegal occupation of East Timor and are widespread throughout Indonesia itself, often as a result of alleged criticism or deviation from the state ideology, *Pancasila*.

When the sale of Alvis tanks and armoured personnel carriers was announced, Amnesty International members questioned the Government about the 'thorough assessment' mentioned in Mr Heseltine's statement in order to evaluate how the Government could guarantee in practice that the sale of these vehicles will not contribute to human rights violations in Indonesia and East Timor. Once again, the government's reply did not disclose any details of the exact criteria and human rights information they considered. It is therefore impossible to judge how the Government came to the conclusion that such a sale would not contribute to the violation of human rights.

Sale of aircraft to Turkey

Gross human rights violations have been inflicted on civilians in southeast Turkey in the context of more than a decade of conflict between Turkish government forces and the Kurdish Workers' Party (PKK). Hundreds of political killings have taken place in the mainly Kurdish southeastern provinces. Dozens of villages have been forcibly evacuated and burned, with numerous villagers 'disappeared' – that is, abducted by agents of the state, while the authorities have denied any knowledge of their whereabouts.

On 26 March 1994, Turkish warplanes and helicopters attacked the Kurdish village of Kumçatï (Kurdish name Besuke). Official statements claimed that the bombing was accidental but the village inhabitants said that they had been subjected to death threats from the security forces because the men in the village had refused to join the village guards – villagers who are armed and paid by the Government to fight guerrillas of the PKK. Five adults and three children were killed in the attack and seventeen children were injured.

On 9 October 1994, it was reported by villagers that Turkish security forces had burned down seventeen villages in eastern Turkey during a three-week offensive against guerrillas. The *Reuters* news agency reported that US-made Sikorsky and Super Cobra helicopters flew over Tunceli town, ferrying in troops and launching rocket attacks. During these operations Ali Karaca, a miller from the village of Ibimahmut, was detained and reportedly tortured near his

EPA Photo

Policeman drags East Timorese student to a police van shortly after dispersing a demonstration by students demanding right to self-determination for people of East Timor

house, then taken away by helicopter. His family found him at Tunceli State Hospital, and reported signs of blows on his body. After three days in a coma, he died. Helicopters and other aircraft have reportedly been used to ferry troops in village raids in which 'disappearances' occurred and to bomb villages. They have also reportedly been used to monitor security operations from the air in which government forces have committed human rights violations.

The Turkish air force made an order in 1993 for a multi-sensor surveillance aircraft (MSSA) from a company called Pilatus Britten-Norman on the Isle of Wight. The MSSA is a Pilatus short take-off and landing aircraft fitted with radar, an infrared optical system and a video/data link. It is listed as having border surveillance and counter-insurgency functions. Britten-Norman was acquired by the Swiss aircraft maker Pilatus in 1979. Pilatus has claimed that its planes are not military equipment, but cases have been documented of its trainer aircraft being modified to provide an offensive military capability. For example, a South Africa-based mercenary agency called Executive Outcomes flew a Swiss Pilatus trainer aircraft on behalf of the Angolan air force (FAPA). The aircraft was fitted with rocket pods and used against UNITA soldiers and civilians. (*International Defense Review,* November 1995). The Pilatus aircraft could clearly, therefore, be used for internal repression.

Amnesty International questioned the Government about what specific human rights criteria it would take into account before sanctioning a licence for the export of military, police or security air-based surveillance equipment to a country that has a poor performance record on protecting human rights. No details were forthcoming. When questioned whether arms supplied to Turkey are being used against the civilian population, the Government stated 'We do not grant licences for the sale of equipment which we believe is likely to be used for internal repression'.

Amnesty International's position

Amnesty International does not oppose arms sales per se, or take a position on the legitimacy of military and economic relations being maintained with countries where human rights are being violated. Amnesty International is, however, opposed to transfers of military, security and police equipment, technology or training which can reasonably be assumed to contribute to human rights violations such as torture, political killings, 'disappearances', arbitrary detentions and unfair trials. In the examples given here, Amnesty International questioned the Government about particular transfers which might contribute to such human rights violations. Because of the human rights situation in these countries, and the type of military or security equipment being proposed for sale, Amnesty International sought assurances from the Government that full consideration of the human rights consequences would be undertaken before any final decision was made about these exports. In each case, the Government failed to provide satisfactory answers. Amnesty International believes that a supplier country has a moral and political duty to demonstrate that its military, security and police transfers will not contribute to human rights violations.

Arms-to-Iraq: the Scott Inquiry
In 1992 Prime Minister John Major set up an inquiry into the 'arms-to-Iraq affair', in which the UK had continued to export military-related equipment during and after the Iran-Iraq war, despite stated Government policy restricting the sale of equipment which could enhance the military capability of either Iran or Iraq. These exports took place against a backdrop of serious human rights violations in Iraq, including summary executions and chemical weapon attacks on Kurdish civilians, which prompted a public and Parliamentary outcry in the UK. The Government deplored the human rights violations occurring in Iraq, but the Scott Inquiry shows that these violations were scarcely considered in the export licensing procedure.

The inquiry, led by Lord Justice Scott, was initiated after the collapse of the trial of Matrix Churchill directors accused of knowingly selling machine tools to Iraq which were designed to make munitions. The directors claimed that the Government knew that their tools were intended for military purposes. Government Ministers signed Public Interest Immunity Certificates to withhold documents such as minutes of meetings and briefings for Government Ministers which might have proved Government

21

knowledge, but the trial judge ordered documents to be released and the trial had to be abandoned. Geoffrey Robertson QC, defence counsel at the trial, commented that in all the documents he had seen relating to the Matrix Churchill exports there was not a single mention of human rights.

The Scott Inquiry reveals that the human rights record of the receiving country is often disregarded because other factors are given greater weight in the process of making decisions about export licences. Firstly there is the protection of intelligence channels which had reported on the likely use of the equipment and would be jeopardised if exports were stopped. There were clear indications that Jordan was acting as a conduit for exports to Iraq, but controls were not widened to include Jordan because of diplomatic ties: the UK Government was reluctant to upset the Jordanian authorities. William Waldegrave, then Minister of State at the Foreign and Commonwealth Office, illustrated the significance given to promotion of UK trade in a note written in 1989:

> 'I doubt if there is any future market of such a scale anywhere where the UK is potentially so well-placed.... We must not allow it to go to the French, Germans, Japanese, Koreans etc....'
> (quoted in Norton-Taylor 1995).

It is clear that there will sometimes be a conflict of interest between the different factors involved in decisions about export licences. But human rights considerations must not be seen as an optional extra.

The Report of the Scott Inquiry was published in February 1996. The Parliamentary and media response to the report concentrated on ministerial accountability and the legal issues surrounding Public Interest Immunity Certificates; human rights scarcely received a mention. One of the less prominent aspects of the Scott Report was its recommendations for a review of the export licence system. Scott made it clear that one purpose of export controls should be 'the avoidance of assistance to human rights abuses in foreign countries' and he questioned the influence of foreign policy issues on export licensing decisions. However, the recommendations included the suggestions that the licensing procedure should be speeded up, with licences receiving approval by default once a specified time limit for processing of applications had expired. Amnesty International would deplore any such step, which could increase the risk of human rights being neglected in the arms control procedure.

What does Amnesty International want?

Amnesty International wants to see the secrecy surrounding arms export procedures lifted. Legislation should be precise, avoiding ambiguities and minimising the scope for contradictory interpretations. It should not, as Alan Clark claimed of the guidelines for exports to Iran and Iraq, be 'obviously drafted with the objective of flexibility in either direction ... offering a form of words elusive of definition' (Norton-Taylor 1995). The Government should prevent transfers of military, security and police equipment from taking place unless it can reasonably demonstrate that they will not contribute to human rights violations. This means providing clear details of human rights criteria and how they are considered in the export-licensing procedure. It also means disclosing details of military, security and police transfers in advance to Parliament.

3 LIFTING THE LID

A call for disclosure of military, security and police transfers

*'It would be difficult to subject defence export licence applications
to public (or Parliamentary) scrutiny, given the need for
commercial confidentiality.'*
David Davis, Minister of State for Foreign and Commonwealth Affairs, letter to
Ken Livingstone MP (7 April 1995).

Secrecy
It is not just the decision-making process which is shrouded in
secrecy as far as export licence applications are concerned. Amnesty
International has continually called for all proposed military,
security and police transfers to be disclosed to Parliament in
advance, to allow scrutiny of proposed exports and to promote
transparency in the export process. Without disclosure, Parliament
has no means to ensure that human rights are protected. The
Government has refused to make public disclosure part of its export
regulations, and several reasons are usually given for this: that there
is no need for such scrutiny; that commercial confidentiality is
required to protect potential sales from competitors; and that the
information cannot be provided due to practical considerations.
These arguments are worth examining in more detail.

Allowing for Parliamentary and public scrutiny
The Government suggests that there is no point in disclosing such
transfers in advance to Parliament. In the words of Richard
Needham, Minister for Trade at the Department of Trade and
Industry:

> 'Each application is subject to careful scrutiny against strict
> criteria. To publish a register of such applications with a view
> to public or Parliamentary debate would simply lead to a
> repetition of this process....'
>
> (letter to William Waldegrave MP, 4 April 1994).

David Davis, Minister of State at the Foreign and Commonwealth, argues further that, in any case:

> 'Parliament can and does question defence export policy by means of Parliamentary Questions, the Foreign Affairs Committee, the Trade and Industry Select Committee and through correspondence by individual Members of Parliament.'
>
> (letter to Toby Jessel MP, 20 July 1995).

The problem with the current system is that MPs have no way of examining whether human rights considerations are properly taken in to account. Because decisions and the decision-making process remain mostly secret, no-one is able even to question the details of the procedure, let alone get information about specific transfers. Despite the claim that Parliament has the opportunity to question military export policy, MPs often cannot get detailed answers to their questions. Indeed as then Prime Minister Margaret Thatcher told the House of Commons in 1987:

> 'Successive governments have agreed that it would not be in the public interest to disclose details of the operation of arms export control procedures.'
>
> (*Hansard*, 13 July 1987).

The UK Government argues further that:

> 'it would pose an intolerable burden on all concerned to submit the 15,000 or so annual export licence applications to Parliament.'
>
> (David Davis, 20 July 1995).

Public disclosure, however, does not have to mean a system where every single application has to receive Parliament's approval. A public register of proposed military, security and police transfers would allow open access to members of Parliament, non-governmental organisations or indeed any individual wishing to examine export policy in general or question a particular licence. Proposed transfers of military, security and police equipment or technology of a high value could be submitted in advance to Parliament, as is the practice in the United States of America.

Commercial confidentiality

The USA has legislation which requires that all proposed foreign military sales over a certain value must be submitted to the US Congress (and therefore placed in the public domain) before they are allowed to proceed. The Congress has between 15 and 30 days to adopt a joint resolution against the proposed sale if there are objections to it, although the President has a veto over this. The receiving country must guarantee not to transfer the equipment to a third country unless it has received the permission of the US President. A variation on such a procedure may provide an appropriate mechanism for UK Parliamentary scrutiny.

Whilst some observers argue that the USA has lost sales because of this open system, it continues to enjoy its position as the world's leading supplier of major conventional weapons. However, the fact that information about military, security and police transfers from the USA is in the public domain at least provides some degree of accountability for Members of Congress, allowing for non-governmental organisations and others interested to scrutinise the USA's system of controls. US legislation also requires the Government to publish annual reports on human rights in the countries it exports to, against which its export licence decisions can be examined. Amnesty International calls on all governments which export military, security and police transfers to issue such reports.

Disproportionate cost

Sometimes the Government does not provide answers to questions asked in Parliament and elsewhere because it is said that the information could only be provided at disproportionate cost or because it is not practicable to extract the information. In the case of export data, it would seem that information could be provided from Customs and Excise records without huge expense. Customs and Excise hold a computer register of export data classifying goods according to nine-digit custom codes. They sell information to a data company for commercial use, but the codes for military, security and police equipment are listed as 'suppressed data'. Since the information exists already, it would not cost more than a small administrative charge to release it, and since the data given does not list company names, commercial confidentiality would not be endangered. Amnesty International believes that full public disclosure of export licence applications in advance is necessary for proper control of military, security and police transfers. The retrospective publication of Customs data however would at least go some way towards achieving transparency. Under the present system it is difficult and time consuming for non-Governmental organisations to gather information on military, security and police exports.

If parliamentarians, non-governmental organisations and other interested parties are allowed to examine UK practice in controlling exports of military, security and police transfers, they could help prevent transfers which might be responsible for human rights violations. The following chapter looks at examples of military, security and police transfers in which public pressure played a key role in trying to protect human rights.

4 PUBLIC INTEREST, PUBLIC PRESSURE

The role of public opinion in military, security and police transfers

'I don't want people in Glasgow knowing that we do this.'

Frank Stott, Director of ICL Technical Plastics, Channel 4 Dispatches, 11 January 1995

On 13 February 1995, Ian Taylor, Parliamentary Under Secretary of State for Trade and Technology, answered a Parliamentary question about applications for export licences to Indonesia which had been refused. His answer began with the familiar: 'It has been the practice of successive Governments not to reveal details of export licences or applications for licences unless the requirements of confidentiality are outweighed by the public interest'. But he went on to say: 'In this instance, I believe that the public interest is served by disclosing the following information,' and gave details of the equipment for which licences were refused. This equipment included riot guns and CS gas cartridges for the Indonesian police. It is not clear how Mr Taylor made his decision to reveal this information, but the intense interest in Indonesia and arms sales (not least from Amnesty International members writing about Hawk jet sales) is likely to have been a factor. The following examples indicate the effect that public knowledge and pressure can have where military, security and police transfers are concerned.

Sale of gallows to United Arab Emirates
A subsidiary of the British building company Laings (company motto: 'We build for people') built three 12-feet high gallows in 1987, to be exported to the United Arab Emirates. Concerned Members of Parliament called on the Government to stop the export, but David Mellor MP, at the time Minister of State at the Foreign and Commonwealth Office, responded that '....the manufacture of execution equipment in the UK is legal and its export is not subject to any form of control'. However, when Laings

were approached they claimed not to have known about the subsidiary's activities, and promised to discontinue the manufacture of the gallows, stating that they were 'concerned to ensure that the good name and reputation of our company.... was not destroyed'. Members of the Furniture, Timber and Allied Trades Union campaigned against the export; and workers at the docks from which the gallows were supposed to be exported helped to ensure that only one of the three sets of gallows ordered was actually sent.

The Scott Inquiry

The Scott Inquiry reveals the significance of public opinion in the arms-to-Iraq affair.

In his report, Lord Justice Scott concluded that 'public opposition in this country might have been embarrassingly vociferous, particularly in view of the use by Iraq of chemical weapons'. The Report recommended that the practice of withholding information on defence-related exports from Parliament be reconsidered. Amnesty International would welcome moves towards a more open and transparent system in which full public debate on military, security and police transfers could take place without the limitations currently imposed by secrecy.

In March 1988 an estimated 5000 people were deliberately killed when Iraqi forces carried out chemical weapon attacks on the town of Halabja in northern Iraq. Government ministers and civil servants were therefore reluctant to publicise the fact that they had just relaxed restrictions on military exports to Iraq. As Mark Higson, former Iraq desk officer at the Foreign and Commonwealth Office, explained to the Scott Inquiry:

> 'We were getting ... tens and tens of letters about the gassing of the Kurds and political prisoners ... It would have been unacceptable to have announced the fact that we were relaxing a policy in favour of Iraq'.

No change in the guidelines on exports to Iraq was announced in Parliament.

Documents made available to the Scott Inquiry show that several civil servants raised their concerns that public opinion would be against the Government's policy on exports to Iraq. However, instead of calling for a restriction to that policy, Foreign and Commonwealth Office official Ian Blackley proposed the very opposite approach in January 1988:

> 'If it becomes public knowledge that the tools are to be used to make munitions, deliveries would have to stop at once. The companies should be warned of the falling guillotine, and urged to produce as fast as they can. They must also renounce publicity and lobbying for their own good'.
>
> (quoted in Norton-Taylor 1995).

Sale of electroshock batons

Amnesty International opposes any transfer of electroshock devices to countries where torture is practised, especially those which have a persistent record of electroshock torture. As well as falling under the remit of export controls, electroshock weapons cannot be possessed, manufactured or traded in the UK without a licence issued under the Firearms Act (1968), follwing a court ruling in 1988.

Broadcast on 11 January 1995, a Channel 4 *Dispatches* documentary, *The Torture Trail*, used secret cameras to gain evidence which indicates that UK companies have supplied and are promoting the sale of electroshock equipment to security forces which practise torture.

Amnesty International has documented testimony of torture victims in countries including China, the Federal Republic of Yugoslavia, Saudi Arabia and Turkey, who say they were tortured with hand-held electroshock devices, including batons and rods. An electric shock from a modern high-pulse stun gun or electroshock baton is designed to incapacitate a human victim. It can cause severe pain and can kill victims with heart disease. A survey by the UK Government's Forensic Science Service in 1990 reported that a one to two second shock from an electroshock stun gun can cause the victim to lose the ability to stand up, and a three to five second shock can induce a total loss of skeletal muscle control producing immobilisation for five to 15 minutes. Victims often feel nauseous and may have convulsions or faint under the shock. Electric shocks with batons are often applied by torturers to sensitive parts of the body, such as the chest, inside of the legs, soles of the feet, inside of the mouth and ears and the genitals.

In China, assaults with electroshock batons are among the most common methods of torture and are reported to occur in virtually all places of detention. On 4 June 1991 Li Jie, a political prisoner in Lingyuan prison, tried to stage a hunger-strike in memory of those killed in Tiananmen Square in 1989. He was dragged to a stage in front of other prisoners, where he was stripped naked, and a 50,000 volt electroshock baton was applied to the inside of his legs by the prison's Brigade Commander. Two other guards applied electro-shock batons to Li Jie's head, neck, shoulders, armpits, chest, stomach and fingers. Li Jie sweated profusely, went into spasms and then became unconscious.

Similar torture and ill-treatment of prisoners in Tibet is reported frequently: according to unconfirmed reports Damchoe Pemo, a Tibetan woman arrested in Lhasa on 20 May 1993, had a miscarriage a week after police forced her to remain standing for at least 12 hours and beat her with electroshock batons.

Still from Dispatches, the Torture Trail

Royal Ordnance employee demonstrates the use of an electroshock baton

The Channel 4 *Dispatches* team filmed undercover with an actor posing as a Middle Eastern arms dealer. They were invited to the premises of Royal Ordnance (part of British Aerospace's Defence Division), where a member of the sales staff claimed that he had arranged for the sale of 8,000 electroshock batons to Saudi Arabia as part of the Al-Yamamah programme (a multi-million pound arms deal between the UK and Saudi Governments). British Aerospace and the Government have denied that this transaction took place. Royal Ordnance did, however, offer to arrange the sale of 10,000 electroshock riot shields and 5,000 electroshock batons from Germany to Lebanon for the undercover actors, withdrawing the offer when the real identity of the *Dispatches* team was revealed.

Amnesty International has received evidence of torture of prisoners with electroshock weapons during 1994 in Lebanon.

Electroshock weapon production line at the Tianjin Bohai Radio Works

The Dispatches programme also filmed the managing director of a Glasgow company called ICL Technical Plastics, who admitted selling electroshock batons to China in 1990 for copy manufacture. He claimed that his sales trip to China was supported by the Department of Trade and Industry. The DTI has denied this. At that time a UK embargo on the sale to China of weapons and equipment which could be used for internal repression was in force.Chinese factories now mass produce electroshock batons.

Despite earlier denials of UK involvement in electroshock exports, in August 1995 the Government admitted, in a written Parliamentary answer to Ann Clwyd MP, that one licence for electroshock batons was issued in 1993. It was a transhipment licence, required when controlled products enter the UK solely for transit to another country. The Government refused to give further details.

Amnesty International local groups and members were among the many who wrote to the Government after the *Dispatches* programme because they were, in the words of one Amnesty

International member, 'utterly dismayed by what it revealed about our trade in weapons of torture'. It would seem likely that, had the proposed export been announced publicly beforehand, public pressure would not have allowed this transfer to take place. Indeed, the director of International Procurement Services, an agent of Royal Ordnance involved in the electroshock trade, claimed to be influenced by public opinion. He wrote to the Kensington & Chelsea Amnesty International UK Group after they held a demonstration outside his offices, stating that although he was formerly an agent for the US-made Nova electronic riot shield, he had 'relinquished this agency as it would appear electronic defence equipment is far too controversial outside of the United States'.

In March 1996, a follow-up *Dispatches* programme was broadcast on Channel 4 entitled *Back on the Torture Trail*. It uncovered five more UK companies who were willing to arrange the sale of electroshock batons, this time to Zaire. They were willing to do this by using weapons manufactured in a third country. One company used a factory in Mexico, the other an 'associate' in South Africa. They could then export the weapons without them ever touching UK soil. This meant that they could evade the UK legal prohibition on possessing, making or exporting electroshock weapons. One Zairean victim of electroshock torture said in the programme: 'They do it to make other people suffer, quite simply to make money'. The shameful fact is that it is legal to sell such equipment provided the shipment does not enter the UK. The programme also revealed that the Government part-funded a document to advise UK firms on 'market opportunities' in the Gulf. One page, in the executive summary, unambiguously provides the market intelligence that 'Qatar: Special Forces are interested in electric batons'. When questioned, the DTI denied responsibility for the document, despite the funding they had provided.

Amnesty International believes advance public disclosure of proposed exports of military, security and police equipment is both necessary and possible, in order that claims that they will not contribute to human rights violations can be properly scrutinised. As Pierre Sané, Secretary General of Amnesty International explains:

'We hope the UK government will move decisively to end the

secrecy, and that Parliamentarians are then able to scrutinize these deals, then take action'.

5 DESTINATION UNKNOWN

Monitoring end use of military, security and police equipment

'It would be impracticable on a regular basis to monitor, after transfer, equipment which we have licensed for export'

Alastair Goodlad, Minister of State for Foreign and Commonwealth Affairs, *Hansard* 19 December 1994

Sale of Hawk jets to Indonesia

Hawk jets sold to Indonesia in the early 1980s are claimed by East Timor's independence movement to have been used in the bombing of civilians in East Timor, though this has been denied by the Indonesian Government.

At the end of 1993 the Indonesian air force announced that it would purchase by 1996 a total of 24 Hawk jets, reportedly equipped with missiles and gun pods, from British Aerospace. Indonesian Air Marshall Sibun and Minister of Research and Technology Jusuf Habibie were reported by *Reuter* and *Antara* news agencies as saying that the planes would be used not only to train pilots, but also for air-to-ground attacks in cases of emergency. According to *The Military Balance 1994-5*, 14 Hawk jets were operating in a counter-insurgency squadron.

Amnesty International UK members contacted MPs about the sale of Hawk jets to Indonesia, requesting that they ask the Government how it will ensure in practice that the Hawk jets will not be used to carry out political killings, particularly since the Indonesian armed forces have been organised principally for internal security purposes. The Government replies made reference to 'assurances' given by the Indonesian authorities, but Amnesty International UK members writing to ask for further clarification of the assurances were not given any details. The Government's response on monitoring was twofold: on the one hand it was claimed that Embassy staff visit East Timor regularly and had not sighted any Hawk jets there, and on the other hand it was argued that 'obviously we cannot

monitor the use of the Hawk aircraft on a regular basis' (Jonathan Aitken, Minister of State for Defence Procurement, letter to Sir John Cope MP, 18 March 1994).

Monitoring the use of military, security and police equipment

Amnesty International believes that the sender must seek to ensure that transfers of military, security and police equipment are not used for human rights abuses. This includes establishing effective mechanisms for monitoring actual end use. At the moment, human rights conditions are not attached to export licences. But legally-binding guarantees about the end use of equipment could be incorporated into the export licence system. Military, security and police exports could also be made conditional upon a right of inspection in the country of final destination. It would, of course, be a mammoth task for UK personnel to monitor directly every single piece of equipment exported. But spot checks are feasible. Reports of misuse could be followed up and thoroughly investigated.

End use documentation

UK legislation requires that most export licence applications must be supported by an international import certificate, and end user statements or end use certificates – the exact requirements vary according to the type of equipment to be exported, the destination and the proposed end use. End use certificates provide information about the ultimate end user of the goods, giving details about their proposed use and assurances about resale or re-export. In the early 1990s, a number of press reports indicated that an illicit trade in false end user certificates was rendering this system of control ineffective. In any case, as Michael Heseltine, then President of the Board of Trade, admitted to the House of Commons in June 1995:

> '....on average, 74 per cent of all applications [for military list licences] during the [1986 to 1989] period did not include the full supporting documentation.... [end user certificates, end use statements or international import certificates].'
>
> (*Hansard,* 13 June 1995)

The importance of supporting documentation was revealed by Customs and Excise officer Chris Berry, who cited one example where an exporter of handgun silencers intended for Colonel Gaddafi's personal guard described his goods as 'sound modifiers for the Libyan Sanitation Department' (*Jane's Defence Weekly,* 28 September 1991). Without supporting documentation there is little opportunity for DTI officials to check the accuracy of statements made on licence applications. Similarly, a UK company registered as an exporter of marine life-saving equipment is listed in Jane's *International Defence Directory* as trading in riot-control grenades, electronic batons, anti-riot weapons and portable explosives – are these being exported under the category of marine equipment? Without close monitoring and transparency there is little way of finding out.

Mr Heseltine put the lack of insistence on supporting documents down to the huge increase in licence applications during the late 1980s and gave assurances that there is now a requirement 'in all cases for a full and unambiguous statement of the intended end use and end user' (*Hansard,* 13 June 1995). However, without effectively monitoring the end use, such statements provide little or no protection of human rights. End use certificates should bind the parties to the contract to observe fundamental human rights.

The Scott Inquiry
The Scott Inquiry once again sheds light on actual past practice in this area. It shows that even when the UK Government has been aware of the end use and destination, little attempt is made to take action to prevent human rights violations.

Firstly, it reveals that the Government was receiving information about the end use of equipment exported from the UK to Iraq. Numerous intelligence reports were filed, and an employee of Matrix Churchill wrote to the Government to raise suspicions that the machine tools would be used to make armaments in Iraq. The information received by the Government indicated that equipment was being used in a way which was contrary to the guidelines on exports to Iraq, but this did not influence the decision-making process. In fact, the Minister for Defence Procurement, Alan Clark, even encouraged companies to list their machine tools as to be used for 'general engineering purposes', avoiding mention of their military application, in order to get through export controls.

Secondly, the Inquiry shows that information about the ultimate destination of exports to Jordan was also ignored. Again, intelligence reports and Customs investigations indicated that Jordan was being used as a first port of call in order to avoid the restrictions on exports to Iraq. A Ministry of Defence official advised the Government of his fears about this diversion, which stemmed not least from his knowledge that Jordan's military forces would be unlikely to order such equipment for its own use. But no extra restrictions were put on exports to Jordan to prevent this circumvention of the export controls. Amnesty International believes that, in order for legislation on military, security and police transfers to be effective in preventing human rights abuses, the legislating body must be provided with all information necessary for it to exercise proper control over the implementation of the law. This should include information about the likely end use and end user of the equipment to be transferred, as well as information about the human rights situation in the receiving country. It would seem that, in the past, the Government has failed to take responsibility for human rights by ensuring that information about the use of military, security and police transfers in practice was received and once received, acted upon.

6 PENALTY FOR IMPROPER USE

Security and police equipment in
human rights abuse

*'With this sort of kit, to be honest I tend not to ask too many
questions about what they're doing with it and where it's going'*
Frank Stott, Director of ICL Technical Plastics, Channel 4 *Dispatches*, 11 January 1995

Misuse of security and police equipment

Sometimes security and police equipment with legitimate uses may
be misused to violate human rights. For example, tear gas could be
argued to have a legitimate use in the open air for certain crowd
control situations. But it can also be used at close quarters in a way
that contributes to human rights violations. In Pakistan, prisoners
and prison warders clashed during a search at Hyderabad Central
Jail on 27 July 1994. A teargas shell was reportedly fired directly into
the face of prisoner Athar Iqbal Arain, smashing his teeth. Although
he was bleeding profusely, Arain was not taken to hospital but
given first aid in the prison dispensary and then reportedly placed
in bar fetters and locked up in an isolation cell. He died in the early
hours of the next morning. The Superintendent and the Chief
Medical Officer of the jail declared that Athar Iqbal Arain had
committed suicide in his cell.

On 29 June 1995, Zimbabwe Police fired CS gas into university
buildings in Harare, including the staff offices, canteen, laboratories,
lecture theatres and halls of residence, during peaceful protests by
students and staff. Over 130 students and staff were reportedly
injured, some seriously. CS gas canisters found after the incident
were identified as having been manufactured by Pains Wessex
(Schermuly) in the UK, and also by a South African company.

Human rights conditions in the receiving country, and the
consequent possibility of misuse of security and police equipment,
should be taken into account by exporters and governments before
transfers of equipment are made to that country. A further example

41

of misuse of civilian equipment took place in China. Shortly after the pro-democracy demonstrations in Tiananmen Square, Beijing on 4 June 1989, *Time* magazine reported that closed-circuit television cameras mounted in the square, purportedly installed as part of a traffic-control system, were used to create 'WANTED posters' of demonstrating students on state-run television and to collect evidence against arrested students and a news correspondent who was then expelled. The surveillance system, called SCOOT, is made by a UK firm and was reportedly purchased partly with World Bank development aid. There have since been reports that cameras have also been installed in the central square in Lhasa, Tibet – a pedestrian area in which Tibetan pro-independence demonstrations are held.

Amnesty International wants an end to the export of any item of security or police equipment to situations where there is evidence that it has been used, or is likely to be used, directly for violating human rights.

New security technology
There is a growing market in riot-control and surveillance equipment, and in new 'non-lethal' technologies. Products include sticky foam, chemical agents such as pepper spray or a combination of the two, plastic and rubber bullets, as well as high pulse electroshock devices including batons, stunguns, shields, fences and belts for prisoners which are remotely operated by prison guards, and darts which can be fired to administer an electric shock from several metres. While the equipment may be designed to incapacitate potentially violent opponents, and is therefore promoted as a non-lethal alternative to firearms, there have been numerous reports of it being misused to commit human rights violations. There have also been reports of deaths associated with some of this equipment.

In the USA a number of people have died after being sprayed with pepper spray (oleoresin capsicum) – a cayenne pepper based substance used by many police departments. There is concern that pepper spray has been a contributing factor in some of these cases. Johnny Williams, a severely disturbed prisoner at a jail in New York

State, died from suffocation in July 1994 during a struggle in which officers sprayed him in the face with three canisters of pepper spray, wrapped a belt around his face and held him down. The cause of death was found to be suffocation through the use of restraints, and a Justice Department inquiry found that the use of pepper spray had been excessive. A 1994 US Government report stated that pepper spray can cause painful burning, eye irritation, coughing, nausea, vomiting and choking when sprayed in a person's face, and warned that pepper gas spray is not only potentially lethal, but capable of causing cancer and birth defects. The UK Government will not allow the police to use these sprays because of fears about their safety, but has not published details of exactly what these fears are. A number of UK companies have expressed a desire to market pepper gas sprays.

Amnesty International believes that governments should be obliged to publish all available independent medical evidence about security products like these before decisions are made about their use or transfer. Effective controls will minimise the risk of ill treatment by law enforcement agencies.

Some US police forces are also equipped with 'Taser' guns which shoot darts that are connected by wires to the gun. The darts then discharge an incapacitating 50,000 volt electric shock into the victim. These darts cause injuries and US police are told that they must be removed by medical personnel. Victims of the excessive use of 'Taser' guns include a mentally disturbed man in handcuffs who died after being 'subdued' by some 20 Los Angeles police officers, who beat him and jolted him repeatedly with a 'Taser' gun. One study published in the US Journal of Forensic Studies concluded that the Taser electric shocks contributed to at least nine out of sixteen Taser-related deaths. Despite dangers like these, 'Taser' guns have still been exported from the USA to Saudi Arabia where Amnesty International has reported electroshock torture.

New technologies like these, designed for law enforcement, are emerging at a rapid rate. Amnesty International believes that if human rights are to be protected there must be tighter legislation to control the use and transfer of these devices.

New security technology

UK companies are amongst those involved in developing and marketing riot-control equipment. A company called Cochrane operating in Birmingham and in South Africa advertises razor wire for 'effective crowd control'. A mobile carrier can dispense 200 metres of razor wire in 15 seconds, providing capacity for the 'capture' of demonstrators. These systems have been sold to Zaire, Taiwan, and Colombia. Cochrane also advertises 'electrocoil': razor wire with an electroshock element of up to 5–7,000 volts built in.

Another UK company, Cray Defence International Ltd, produces a Talon Internal Security Vehicle, which incorporates electrified side panels to repulse demonstrators. A UK company called Amac Corporation tried to export similar vehicles to Chile in 1984, but the Government made it clear that it would be very unlikely to issue an export licence for the sale. Nevertheless, Cray Defence International still saw fit to invest £1 million in developing its product.

With technological developments moving quickly, there is a danger that they will outstrip legal controls. The list classifying the types of equipment which require export licences may not include sensitive new security equipment. Governments and companies need to be vigilant about supplies of such equipment and technology in order to prevent transfers which contribute to human rights violations. In calling for transparency and tighter legislation, Amnesty International is trying to safeguard people's human rights from the abuses for which these technological advances could be used.

7 OILING THE WHEELS

Practical support for military, security and police transfers

The Government's system of control operated under the Export of Goods (Control) Order can sometimes fail to prevent military, security and police transfers which are likely to contribute to human rights violations, either because of inadequacies in its implementation or because companies set out to evade controls.

Otokar – Landrover Exhibition at IQEF, a military exhibition held in Turkey. September 1995

S. Wright

This chapter examines the ways in which UK companies can profit from military, security and police trade by exploiting loopholes in the current legislation to avoid official export controls.

Licensed production

One way in which export controls are avoided is by the licensing of products for manufacture abroad.

Since 1987 a Turkish company called Otobus Karoseri Sonayi AS ('Otokar') has assembled Land Rovers under licence from its UK parent company for sale to military and civilian markets in Turkey. In 1994 production began in Turkey of a new type of Land Rover, a light reconnaissance armoured vehicle with machine-gun mount, using imported automotive parts, and designed for transporting troops for counter-insurgency and light attack. About 2,500 will be assembled per year for use by the Turkish army and security forces.

Amnesty International is concerned because it has documented cases where this type of vehicle has been used in committing human rights violations.

Much of the civilian population in southeast Turkey lives in constant fear of random violence and being caught in reprisal killings. On 13 September 1994 Bedri Tan, father of eight and headman of the village of Kad köy (Kurdish name Qadiya) was detained at his home by gendarmes. According to his family, he was taken into a separate room in the house, interrogated under torture, and taken away in a Gendarmerie Land Rover. On 14 September Bedri Tan's family received a telephone call from the Gendarmerie Headquarters telling them to collect his body, which had been dismembered.

Turkish security forces were filmed driving an armoured personnel carrier (in this case a vehicle made in the USA) into a crowd in the town of Cizre in March 1993. The soldiers were seen striking an unarmed man and beating his head against the vehicle before driving him away. On 11 September 1993, following a clash in Cizre between guerillas and security forces, a curfew was announced and armoured vehicles patrolled the streets firing indiscriminately. Two children were killed.

According to answers received by Amnesty International UK

members via their MPs about the use of Land Rovers in Turkey, the Government has no role in the procedure for licensing the manufacture in other countries of such equipment. No licence is required for the export of automotive parts from the UK as they are not specifically designed for military use, and while export controls do in theory cover the transfer of military and security technology, it appears that the Government did not consider the controls to be applicable in this case. Ian Taylor, Parliamentary Under-Secretary of State for Trade and Technology, explained that it is up to the commercial judgement of companies whether to enter into arrangements for production overseas under licence (letter to Jim Marshall MP, 28 November 1994). But when Land Rover was approached about the Otokar arrangement the Managing Director explained that:

> .... in terms of sales of our products we accept Government guidance ... we have no idea whether a car might be used for Government, military, police or other purpose.... it would be administratively impossible to insist on knowing the end use of every car before it was sold. It is against this background that we feel we have neither the right nor the basis on which to reach conclusions and must, therefore, rely on our own national Government, or other recognised bodies ... to provide the necessary guidance'.
> (letter to Amnesty International member, 16 November 1993).

Amnesty International calls for both companies and governments to take responsibility for their military, security and police transfers. Whilst governments have ultimate responsibility for safeguarding human rights, this does not absolve companies or individuals from ensuring that they do not contribute to human rights abuses.

The Turkish company Otokar is now exporting its vehicles to other countries. The *Turkish Defence and Aerospace* newsletter for July/August 1995 describes how Otokar, having successfully established itself as supplier to the Turkish Armed Forces, has signed contracts to export its Land Rover-based vehicles to Pakistan. It is also reported to have exported 100 such vehicles to Algeria.

Transfers remaining outside the UK

Another way of avoiding export controls, practised by a number of UK companies, is by 'brokering' transfers so that the goods are never physically imported to or exported from the UK. Private dealers and Government agencies can arrange deals where both supplier and purchaser remain outside the UK. No UK regulations apply if the equipment itself remains outside the UK, even if the UK benefits financially from such deals. The controls only cover equipment that is actually exported from the UK. There are reported to be over 300 arms dealers in London alone, as well as foreign government agencies. As Sir Geoffrey Howe explained in July 1987:

The organisation of transactions in arms sales is not illegal unless the goods concerned are imported into or exported from the United Kingdom in breach of British law'.

(*Hansard*, 21 July 1987).

Compass Safety International, one of the companies investigated in the *Dispatches* documentary *Back on the Torture Trail* (1996),

S. Duponta

Civilian casualties, Rwanda, injured at MSF Hospital, Byumba

explained how easy it was to get round UK export controls. They would simply arrange a shipment of electroshock batons from their supplier in Mexico direct to the buyer without the batons ever entering the UK.

In June 1995 Amnesty International published a report (see Appendix III) raising its concerns at evidence that the perpetrators of crimes against humanity in Rwanda between April and July of the previous year, now in exile in Zaire, were receiving large supplies of weapons and ammunition. Some of this equipment had been used by the former Rwandese Armed Forces and the *Interahamwe* militia for cross-border incursions from Zaire into Rwanda, where political killings took place. Amnesty International was concerned that the transfer of military equipment to these exiled forces was likely to result in further human rights abuses and therefore should be prevented. An embargo on arms sales to Rwanda was imposed by the United Nations in May 1994. Amnesty International does not support or oppose embargoes or sanctions, but does oppose military, security and police transfers to military, paramilitary or security units which are responsible for human rights violations.

The reports of small arms transfers investigated by two UK television programmes (*The Big Story*, November 1994 and The *Cook Report*, June 1995), included admissions of involvement in a series of secret flights carrying arms to Goma in Zaire from several countries, including Albania, Israel and Bulgaria. These were reported to have been arranged by traders in the UK using aircraft registered in Ghana, Nigeria, Ukraine and Russia, without the arms ever entering the UK. Amnesty International urged the governments concerned and the United Nations to investigate these allegations in order to protect human rights. The Bulgarian, Ghanaian and Nigerian Governments denied the allegations; UK Customs and Excise (which is responsible for policing export controls) undertook to investigate the reports of UK involvement, but no prosecutions have been initiated. A UN commission of inquiry reported in 1996 that there were strong indications that aircraft were continuing to land in Zaire with arms for the former Rwandan government forces.

Amnesty International calls on governments to enact legislation and regulations which will prevent their nationals from engaging in

foreign licensed production agreements or 'offshore' trading
agreements where these can reasonably be assumed to contribute
to human rights violations.

8 HUMAN RIGHTS EDUCATION?

Military, security and police training and personnel

The UK is one of a number of states which provide training to military and police personnel from many countries, including some which display systematic patterns of human rights abuse. Amnesty International believes that all such training should include a human rights component involving practical exercises. Candidates should only be selected from security forces which are subject to an effective system of accountability for human rights.

Military training

In 1995 the Government provided military training for the forces of some 106 countries. Some of this training was provided by UK personnel going overseas, while some was carried out at military training establishments in the UK. A list of the countries involved can be found in Appendix I.

In response to a Parliamentary Question about such military training, Nicholas Soames MP, Minister of State for the Armed Forces, indicated that the Government would prefer details about the military training of personnel from overseas to be kept secret:

'It is not normally our practice to disclose the precise details of military training given to any particular country as such details are regarded as being confidential between governments. There are no plans to change this policy.'

(*Hansard*, 28 March 1995).

Sometimes, UK military or police training has contributed to the violation of human rights in the receiving country. In the past, UK training has been implicated in human rights violations. One example is Cambodia, where British army teams (allegedly from the SAS) ran intensive courses in sabotage and mine laying for Cambodian opposition groups in the 1980s, which contributed to political killings. According to the UK Mines Advisory Group which

52

interviewed a number of the participants, the SAS trainers taught the Cambodian non-communist armed opposition commanders to place anti-personnel mines in unmarked wells, water sources and track junctions, as well as to use booby traps with mines. Internally displaced civilians were thereby targeted – there were deaths and serious injuries such as those sustained at the massacre at Sala Kraw camp on 19 February 1991 which was reported by the International Committee of the Red Cross.

Foreign and Commonwealth Office Minister Douglas Hogg, in a letter to AIUK Grantham Group about military training stated that : 'I do not agree that the fact that we have provided such training implies UK responsibility for any subsequent abuses' (26 May 1994). But Amnesty International calls on all governments which provide military, security and police training to accept responsibility for the human rights impact of such training. Allegations that human rights violations are linked to such training must be investigated and the results of the investigation made public.

At the end of 1993 Amnesty International UK local groups wrote to the Government about the training provided by UK personnel to the new army in Mozambique (formed by the merging of the Mozambican Government and Renamo forces after the signing of the General Peace Agreement in October 1992). They asked whether the instructors training the Mozambican armed forces had themselves received human rights training and requested details of the training they were providing. In Amnesty International's view, it was essential to ensure that adequate provisions were made for protecting human rights during the peace process in Mozambique which ended the 15-year civil war in 1992. These provisions should include practical ways to ensure that military personnel of all ranks are made aware of their obligations to uphold human rights.

In reply, Baroness Chalker, Minister of State at the Foreign and Commonwealth Office, stated:

'We fully agree on the need to promote human rights as an integral part of the training programme. We believe that training is a positive way to promote good government and respect for human rights, and that it is likely to help reduce the level of human rights abuses. All the trainees in Mozambique receive at

least one lecture devoted to human rights questions. The instructors' course at Nyanga included instruction in the laws of armed conflict and the terms of the Geneva Convention'
(letter to Roy Hattersley MP, 22 June 1994).

Amnesty International welcomes the inclusion (if limited) of human rights and international humanitarian law in this training and the fact that local Amnesty International groups were told about it. However, Amnesty International is concerned that the Government will not reveal details about the human rights content of all of the training it offers. Amnesty International would like all police and military training provided by the UK to include human rights instruction, and to be open to public scrutiny so that the content and scope of any human rights instruction included is made clear.

Police training

Between 1991 and 1995, the UK provided training for police forces of 64 countries which took place in the form of 157 visits to police forces in the UK (for a list of countries involved, see Appendix II). Other training was provided by UK visits overseas, such as the secondment of seven police officers to Nigeria over the same period (*Hansard*, 4 December 1995). Amnesty International is concerned that police training should always include instruction in measures to protect human rights in accordance with international law.

In 1990, the Government listed Nigeria as one of a number of countries which has sent delegations of police to the UK to study crowd control techniques (*Hansard*, 2 February 1990) and in 1995 an answer to a Parliamentary Question stated that training of Nigerian police in the UK in 1990 and 1991 had included maintenance of public order (*Hansard*, 19 December 1995). The Nigerian police force is routinely implicated in human rights violations, including killings which have taken place during pro-democracy demonstrations in Nigeria's cities, for example during riots in Lagos on 18 July 1994. Reportedly, some of those killed were not involved in violent activities or posing a threat to the police. Amnesty International is concerned to know what, if any, element of human rights was involved in the training in crowd control techniques given by the UK to the Nigerian police force and to police in other countries.

Financial support for training

As well as providing training to other countries, the UK provides financial assistance for its military and police training. For example, the Foreign and Commonwealth Office operates the UK Military Training Assistance Scheme. In the financial year 1994–5 the cost of this scheme was estimated to be around £12 million. In addition, the Ministry of Defence often agrees to waive the costs of training provided to foreign governments; in 1994–5 these waivers were in the region of £5.6 million (Hansard 9 and 11 May 1995). Amnesty International calls on the Government to give details of the human rights training courses and systems of accountability governing the trainees for which this financial support is provided. This will help ensure that the Government does not contribute to human rights violations.

Advertisement for E-29 Research Group's training in counter insurgency techniques

Private companies and mercenaries

Private companies registered in the UK are also involved in training overseas military, security and police forces. For example, a UK company based in London called E-2G Research Group provides training in counter-insurgency, low-intensity conflict and internal security to foreign forces. Do the techniques they teach conform to international human rights standards? Without transparency, there is no way of knowing. Details about UK training can usually only be gleaned through other means such as eyewitness accounts and media reports.

In 1995 a number of press reports indicated that companies based in the UK were involved in assisting the government of Sierra Leone in its conflict with rebel forces. The conflict in Sierra Leone between the insurgent Revolutionary United Front (RUF) and government soldiers, which has been fought since 1991, has been characterised by abuses committed by both sides against defenceless civilians in their homes, villages and towns. Government soldiers have been responsible for unlawful killings of unarmed civilians and for torture, ill-treatment and extrajudicial execution of captured rebels. People accused of collaborating or sympathising with rebel forces, sometimes on the basis of little or no evidence, have also been tortured, ill-treated and summarily executed. In January 1996, two RUF fighters captured at Lunsar, Northern Province were summarily decapitated by government troops and 15 rebels captured in the Bo area of Southern Province in September 1995 were reported to have been publicly executed by the army.

A UK company called Gurkha Security Guards, based in the Channel Islands, was reported by *InterPress Service* in April 1995 to be recruiting former British soldiers from the Gurkha regiment on behalf of the Sierra Leonean government. In addition, a South African company, Executive Outcomes, reportedly operating from the UK, was said to have sent in 150 soldiers, including former mercenaries and members of the special units of the South African Defence Force (*Observer*, 15 August 1995). In both cases it was claimed that the foreign soldiers were only present as trainers and advisers, and not involved in front-line combat, but reports from Sierra Leone indicate that soldiers employed by Executive Outcomes have also been directly involved in the fighting (see *International Defence Review*, November 1995).

According to the report by *InterPress Service* (27 April 1995), a Foreign and Commonwealth Office spokesperson said that 'if people who are no longer in the British Army decide to sell their services elsewhere we cannot stop them'. Once again, the Government effectively turns a blind eye to potential ways in which the UK contributes to human rights abuses elsewhere in the world. Amnesty International believes that the Government has a responsibility to ensure that military training or other security assistance provided by private companies to those involved in the conflict in Sierra Leone (or elsewhere) includes human rights safeguards and does not facilitate human rights abuses. The United Nations adopted a *Convention Against the Recruitment, Use, Financing and Training of Mercenaries* in 1989, which requires signatory states to abstain from recruiting, financing or training mercenaries and to enact laws to prohibit such activities. But the Government has not signed the Convention and has no plans to do so, arguing that it would be difficult to implement under UK law.

UK law makes no provision with regard to mercenarism and the protection of human rights. An act of law dating back to last century, the *Foreign Enlistment Act* (1870), prohibits British subjects from becoming mercenaries and recruiting others to do so, but there are doubts about its applicability in modern circumstances. For example, it defines the offence of leaving the UK to enlist as a mercenary by reference only to departure by ship, so that leaving by air would not be unlawful. The Act has never been used for a prosecution in connection with enlistment or recruitment, but it has been invoked as a threat on several occasions in an attempt to prevent British citizens becoming mercenaries in particular conflicts. A commission of inquiry led by Lord Diplock in 1976 found that the Act was unworkable and recommended that future legislation should concentrate on prohibiting recruitment rather than making enlistment illegal. However, no new legislation has been drawn up.

Amnesty International is opposed to transfers of military personnel which contribute to human rights violations in its mandate such as political killings and torture. Such violations may occur where personnel are encouraged to operate outside the accepted systems of accountability which are based on international humanitarian and human rights law. When a party to an armed conflict hires mercenaries, this is the kind of situation which may arise. Furthermore, mercenaries often commit human rights violations such as extrajudicial executions where they are discouraged from taking prisoners of war, or when they have been rewarded according to a 'kill-rate'.

9 'BATTING FOR BRITAIN'

Promotion of UK trade in military, security and police transfers

'Whenever Mrs Thatcher or Mr Major comes back, having batted for Britain and won a great deal, everyone says Hooray! They are heroes on the front page'

William Waldegrave, former Foreign and Commonwealth Office Minister, evidence to the Scott Inquiry, quoted in Norton-Taylor 1995

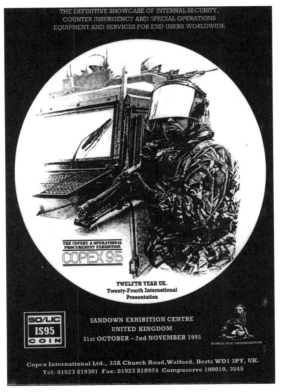

Advertisement for Copex 1995

One of the purposes of military training by the UK is made clear in a Foreign and Commonwealth Office Departmental Report of 1994. The section concerning the UK's Military Training Assistance Scheme states that training 'also encourages these individuals [the recipients] to look to the UK when.... purchasing equipment'. But under the enormous pressure to secure arms sales, human rights can be overlooked.

The Government gives UK companies which manufacture and trade in military and security equipment enormous assistance with the export promotion of their products. The Defence Export Services Organisation (DESO), part of the Ministry of Defence, has nearly 700 staff, including some posted overseas, who help UK manufacturers market and sell their products abroad. DESO can advise on defence markets, provide military assistance in support of sales, provide advice on export finance, help to organise exhibitions of military equipment and assist in government to government sales. The Department of Trade and Industry (DTI) also provides grants towards the cost of UK companies exhibiting security equipment abroad.

Numerous exhibitions of military, security and police equipment are held every year all over the world. Several are held in the UK, including the annual Covert and Operational Procurement Exhibition (COPEX) and the biennial Royal Navy and British Army Equipment Exhibition (RN&BAEE). The 1995 RN&BAEE was attended by official delegations from countries where security forces are known to have committed persistent human rights violations, including Angola, Chile, Indonesia, Kenya, Mexico and Sri Lanka.

COPEX 1994, held in the UK, was visited by official country delegations including Iran (even though the UK had announced a complete military ban on Iran at the time), Turkey, Saudi Arabia, Colombia, Algeria, South Korea and China. COPEX 1995 was attended by a large delegation of the Indonesian military unit Kopassus, which has been notorious for its perpetration of human rights violatons. The possession or marketing of electroshock weapons has been illegal in the UK without a firearms licence since 1988, but among the exhibitors at COPEX 1992 was a US/Hungarian company which, according to the exhibition catalogue, marketed 'electric shocking devices'; leaflets advertising its electroshock products were available at the exhibition. The *Dispatches* undercover team which filmed at COPEX 1994 met company representatives there who were willing to discuss the sale of electroshock weapons. Potential exhibitors at COPEX 1995 in Bonn, Germany, which was cancelled after protests, included a number of companies who list electroshock equipment amongst their products. In a press release issued in Germany the exhibition organisers stated that 'COPEX does not exhibit torture instruments or electroshock batons'.

Amnesty International believes that representatives of security forces which are known to carry out human rights violations should not be invited to attend exhibitions that promote the sale of security equipment and technology. Moreover, the names of official guests and companies exhibiting, the products and services exhibited, and any proposed sale or transfer arising from such exhibitions should be made public.

Financial support for transfers

Enormous financial support is also given by the Government to encourage transfers of military, security and police equipment. The Export Credits Guarantee Department (ECGD) provides insurance for exporters, covering their costs if the buyer is unable to pay. The ECGD gave guarantees for defence business in the years 1990–95 worth around £5000 million (*Hansard,* 5 April 1995); one estimate of the actual cost to the ECGD of backing arms sales is £300 million a year (World Development Movement, 1995).

Amnesty International does not take a position on the legitimacy of providing such finance, or maintaining any military, economic or cultural relations with governments or opposition groups who practise human rights violations. However, in Amnesty International's view, human rights protection requires not only that there be proper export controls of military, security and police equipment, training and personnel' but that controls using human rights criteria should also apply to decisions about the financing of these transfers. At present, the mechanisms for doing this are extremely opaque, and fundamentally inadequate.

10 *THE WORLDWIDE AGENDA*

International controls on military, security and police transfers

'The truth is that human rights violations have no borders. The fight against human rights violations can only be international'
Pierre Sané, Secretary General of Amnesty International, keynote speech at Liberty Human Rights Convention, 16 June 1995

The need for international controls

In August 1991, hundreds of Heckler and Koch sniper rifles and machine guns were found at the *Stasi* (State Security Service) office in Berlin. An investigation by German government prosecutors found that, to evade West German controls on military and security transfers to East Germany, the weapons had been shipped in parts to Royal Ordnance in the UK, then re-assembled and re-exported using false UK export licences (specifying Colombia) to Rostock, a city then in East Germany. A German court was told in 1994 that the same network was used for shipments to Central America and the Middle East.

In 1993 the Swiss government granted a licence to the aircraft company Pilatus to export twenty PC-9 aircraft to South Korea. But just in case the licence was refused, Pilatus had been making contingency arrangements to build the aircraft in Germany in order to evade a Swiss ban. In 1994, Pilatus announced that it planned to move production of some of its other aircraft to its subsidiary Britten-Norman on the Isle of Wight (the company making surveillance aircraft for Turkey – see Chapter Two). It was reported in *Flight International* (6 April 1994), and *The Observer* (24 March 1994) that this was in order to get around Swiss controls on the export of military equipment to areas of war or tension. Shortly after, Pilatus was indeed refused a licence to export to Mexico by the Swiss government following the use of Pilatus aircraft in armed conflict in the Chiapas region. The aircraft had been exported for civilian use. We can only wonder if the UK Government would make the same decision if asked to grant a licence for Britten-Norman. With no international co-ordination of licensing procedure, there is no way of ensuring that they take the same decision as the Swiss Government.

After a US Senate decision to curb sales of small arms to Indonesia on human rights grounds, the Indonesian government was reported as saying that it would look for other sources for small arms, such as the UK (*International Security Digest*, July 1994).

These examples indicate that unless effective international, multilateral controls of military, security and police transfers are in operation, then transfers will continue to take place even if individual governments have properly exercised control over those exports which could contribute to human rights violations.

The Government has supported several statements on arms export control at European level and wider.

European Union Common Criteria for Arms Exports
The European Union Council of Ministers agreed the *Common Criteria for Arms Exports* at its European Council meetings in Luxembourg, 1991, and Lisbon, 1992. The eight Criteria should form the basis of any future common policy on arms exports. The Criteria include 'the respect of human rights in the country of final destination' and 'the behaviour of the buyer country with regard to .... respect for international law'. In addition, they stipulate consideration of 'the existence of a risk that equipment will be diverted within the buyer country or re-exported under undesirable conditions'.

However, these Criteria are not binding, and governments interpret them differently. As David Davis, Minister of State at the Foreign and Commonwealth Office, explained in April 1995:

'We regularly discuss with our European partners possible steps towards a common policy but given the close relationship between arms sales and national foreign and security interests we have yet to agree a single policy'.

(letter to Keith Mans MP, 7 April 1995)

In order to build an effective system internationally to protect human rights, European Union Member States need, at the very least to implement these Criteria urgently within the framework of their Common Foreign and Security Policy. A group of non-governmental organisations has produced a European Code of Conduct on the Arms Trade which defines how each of the Common Criteria for arms exports could be implemented. This Code could form a basis for legislative controls. For example, the criterion 'respect of human rights in the country of final destination' has been defined and clarified in the Code in terms of international law in order to help the government of the exporting country to ensure that its exports do not contribute to human rights violations.

Amnesty International supports the commitment to human rights outlined in this proposed Code of Conduct and welcomes its call for public disclosure and mechanisms to monitor end use guarantees. Amnesty International also welcomes the definition of 'transfers' in the Code which includes not only military but also security and police equipment, training and logistical support.

Amnesty International wishes to ensure that any process of harmonising arms export control internationally should lead to the highest possible level of control in terms of human rights criteria. It should not be a process of 'watering-down' controls to suit the lowest common denominator. European Union governments should ensure that a transparent decision-making procedure is in place, with effective Parliamentary control. They should also jointly suspend military, security and police transfers to countries which can reasonably be assumed to contribute to human rights violations, so that action by one EU government to protect human rights is not overridden by another EU country making the transfer instead.

Regulation on Dual-Use Goods
The European Union has adopted a *Regulation on the Control of Exports of Dual-Use Goods and Technologies* which came into force in July 1995. 'Dual-use goods' is the term used to describe equipment which is capable of, but not specifically designed for, military purposes. This includes certain computers, electronic and instrumentation equipment, machine tools, chemicals, transport and communications equipment and radar. This Regulation defines the

type of dual-use equipment which is subject to EU controls and the countries for which less strict controls are required (NATO countries, Australia, etc.). It allows the exporter to impose conditions of export, for example concerning the end use or re-export of the equipment. Member states who refuse to issue a licence or decide to revoke one are required to inform other member states of this decision.

However, the Regulation provides guidelines for decisions on whether an export should be allowed; the guidelines include consideration of the 1991-2 Common Criteria for Arms Exports, and considerations about intended end use and the risk of diversion to another country. There is no explicit mention of human rights criteria in the Regulation, and the requirements for end use checks are vague. Amnesty International believes full and stringent human rights criteria should be included in this Regulation as well as requirements for the proper monitoring of the end use of all dual-use products.

Principles Governing Conventional Arms Transfers

The Government has also supported statements, similar to the European Union's Common Criteria for Arms Exports, by the Organisation for Security and Co-operation in Europe (OSCE) and by the Five Permanent Members of the United Nations Security Council. The fifty-four states of the OSCE agreed the Principles Governing Conventional Arms Transfers (adopted in Rome in November 1993) which also refer to respect for human rights in the recipient country: *'Each participating state will avoid transfers which would be likely to be used for the violation or suppression of human rights and fundamental freedoms'*.

The Guidelines for Conventional Arms Transfers agreed by the Five Permanent Members (China, France, Russia, UK, USA) in October 1991 do not mention human rights specifically, but they do propose the refusal of arms transfers which would be likely to be used other than for the legitimate defence and security needs of the recipient state. Like the European Union's Common Criteria, these principles and guidelines are not incorporated into domestic law and remain open to individual governments' interpretation. Amnesty

International believes that such human rights principles need to be explicitly included in all national and international controls on military, security and police transfers. The Government could play a significant part in achieving this, had it the political will to do so.

United Nations Register of Conventional Arms

The Government helped the United Nations to establish a Register of Conventional Arms in 1991 to increase international transparency in weapons transfers. However, the Register covers just seven categories of large conventional weapons: battle tanks; armoured combat vehicles; large calibre artillery systems; combat aircraft; attack helicopters; warships; missiles and missile launchers. It fails to include categories of light weapons which are used significantly in human rights violations. The Register is also voluntary and retrospective, each country making a submission on the previous year's imports and exports. The first data on 1992 was submitted by April 1993 and the Register was published for the first time in October 1993.

By the time the UN published its 1995 report, eighty-four countries had submitted data for 1994, including 14 of the 15 largest exporters for that year and 11 of the 15 largest importers, as classified by the Stockholm International Peace Research Institute. Participation from countries in the Middle East, sub-Saharan Africa, Latin America and the former Soviet Union has, however, been poor.

As it stands at the moment, the Register is of limited use with respect to monitoring the export of weapons which may be used for grave human rights abuses, since many political killings, 'disappearances', torture and arbitrary arrests are carried out using light weapons and security equipment, which are not included in the Register. Amnesty International believes that if these categories of equipment were included in the UN Register of Conventional Arms, the increased international transparency would improve steps taken to protect human rights.

The Wassenaar Arrangement

Most recently, in April 1996, the Government became a party to a new international arms control agreement involving all the NATO member states as well as Russia and some others. The Wassenaar Arrangement on Export Controls for Conventional Arms and Dual-Use Goods and Technologies is designed to replace the system of arms and dual-use technologies – originally established in 1949 – which NATO directed against the former Soviet Union. At present the Wassenaar Arrangement is focused on preventing the proliferation of technologies used in weapons of mass destruction and the build up of very large stocks of conventional weapons as categorized by the UN Register of Conventional Arms. However, there are no binding regulations and no attempt to monitor or control the proliferation of small arms or light weapons, despite proposals by some governments to introduce such measures. These must be introduced if the Wassenaar Arrangement is to be instrumental in preventing human rights abuses by controlling arms and technologies.

CONCLUSION

The indiscriminate proliferation of weapons and potentially harmful technologies which fuel human rights violations is not in anyone's interest. This book has examined the UK's involvement in the trade in military, security and police equipment, training and personnel. It has shown that the Government has failed to establish an effective and transparent mechanism in order to take human rights fully into consideration before authorizing such transfers. It has also shown that current export controls can be evaded. Even where legislation and guidelines would in theory prevent transfers which are used in committing human rights violations, the implementation of these controls has not always ensured the proper protection of human rights. Amnesty International is pressing the Government to demonstrate its commitment to human rights by making its controls on military, security and police transfers conform more strictly to human rights criteria. The laws and procedures governing these transfers should be made more transparent to allow for public scrutiny and the Government should take a lead to promote better international controls.

Amnesty International's Recommendations

Amnesty International calls for legislative and other measures, both at UK and international level, which would prohibit military, security and police transfers from taking place unless it can be reasonably demonstrated in each case that a transfer will not contribute to human rights violations, including the detention of prisoners of conscience, torture or other cruel, inhuman or degrading treatment of prisoners; unfair trials, extrajudicial executions, the death penalty, indiscriminate killings and 'disappearances'. Similar controls should prevent military, security and police transfers from reaching armed opposition groups where it is reasonable to assume that these would contribute to hostage-taking, torture or deliberate killing.

The government should undertake changes to current export controls so that:

- all military, security and police transfers, including those arranged from the UK where equipment remains outside the country, are disclosed in advance to Parliament.

- human rights in the intended receiving country are taken into consideration before any decision to approve a transfer;
- reports are issued on the human rights situation in receiving countries;
- Parliament is notified of all information necessary to enable it to exercise proper control over the implementation of the law, including information on human rights from non-governmental organisations;
- all military and security exhibitions are required to publish guest lists, names of exhibitors, products and services on display and no visas or invitations are issued to representatives of security forces known to carry out human rights violations;
- the Government effectively monitors the end use of military, security and police transfers and includes human rights criteria in all end use certificates;
- the sender takes responsibility for the stated use of military, security and police transfers in practice, for example by making future contracts dependent on adherence to human rights criteria;
- all international mechanisms for transparency and control include light weapons and security equipment.

The European Union and the OSCE member states should:

- effectively implement the Common Criteria for Arms Exports and the Principles Governing Conventional Arms Transfers;
- work together to prevent military, security and police transfers which would contribute to human rights violations, so that preventive action by one member state is not undermined by companies or buyers taking advantage of another state's laxer controls.

What you can do
In the past, public pressure has helped to achieve changes in legislation and prevent transfers taking place. The Amnesty International UK members and local groups who have campaigned

on this issue helped to secure the inclusion of leg-irons, shackles and gang-chains in the Export of Goods (Control) Order and thereby prevent human rights abuses. Trade unionists helped to prevent the export of gallows to the United Arab Emirates. Investigative journalists have helped focus public attention on the trade in electroshock weapons. Parliamentarians can be encouraged to take an active role in helping to ensure effective controls; already some members of the UK and European Parliaments whose constituents have raised this issue have helped to campaign for changes in the law, with nearly 200 MPs signing an Early Day Motion in 1995, calling for public disclosure and proper Parliamentary control of military, security and police transfers. Your efforts can help to secure similar successes in the future.

You can help the campaign for better controls on military, security and police transfers by:

Writing to your local MP – Express your concern about this issue, and ask your MP to press the Government to end the secrecy surrounding military, security and police transfers. Ask him or her to raise the need for Parliament to make the changes outlined above in order to establish effective controls in the UK and internationally;

Writing to your MEP – Ask him or her to raise your concerns in the European Parliament and to join the campaign for safeguards and controls based on human rights. Point out that the Common Criteria need to be effectively implemented at EU level and by all EU States;

Raising the matter in organisations to which you belong – such as a local political party, trade union branch, religious or community group. Encourage members to write, both as a group and individually, to local MPs and MEPs, and raise awareness in your community by organising a talk, writing to the local newspaper or passing motions of support for the new measures called for by Amnesty International.

Joining Amnesty International – and helping our efforts to identify the companies and organisations responsible for the export of military, security and police equipment and training to countries where they may be used for the violation of human rights. Information about the trade often comes to Amnesty International from sources such as members of the public, students and journalists.

APPENDIX I

UK Foreign Military Training

Military personnel from the following countries either visited the UK to receive military training or were visited by UK military personnel in 1995.

Albania
Antigua
Australia
Austria
Bahrain
Bahamas
Bangladesh
Barbados
Belarus
Belgium
Belize
Bermuda
Botswana
Brazil
British Virgin Islands
Brunei
Bulgaria
Canada
Cayman Islands
Chile
Colombia
Cyprus
Czech Republic
Denmark
Dominican Republic
Ecuador
Egypt
El Salvador
Estonia
Falkland Islands
Fiji
Finland
France
Germany
Ghana
Greece
Grenada
Guatemala

Guyana
Hong Kong
Hungary
India
Indonesia
Ireland
Israel
Italy
Ivory Coast
Jamaica
Japan
Jordan
Kenya
Kuwait
Kyrghistan
Latvia
Lebanon
Lesotho
Lithuania
Macedonia
Malaysia
Maldives
Malta
Malawi
Mauritius
Mexico
Moldova
Montserrat
Morocco
Mozambique
Namibia
Nepal
Netherlands
New Zealand
Norway
Oman
Pakistan
Paraguay

Philippines
Poland
Portugal
Qatar
Romania
Russia
Rwanda
St Kitts-Nevis
St Lucia
St Vincent
Saudi Arabia
Senegal
Seychelles
Sierra Leone
Singapore
Slovakia
Slovenia
South Africa
South Korea
Spain
Sri Lanka
Swaziland
Sweden
Switzerland
Tanzania
Thailand
Trinidad and Tobago
Turks and Caicos Islands
Turkey
United Arab Emirates
Uganda
Ukraine
USA
Venezuela
Zambia
Zimbabwe

Source: Hansard.
30 Nov 1995

APPENDIX II:

Police Training

Countries which received police training in the UK between January 1991 and November 1995 (one visit unless number specified):

Antigua
Argentina
Aruba
Australia
Bahrain (8)
Bahamas
Bangladesh (2)
Barbados (3)
Bermuda (4)
Bolivia
Botswana (5)
Brunei (2)
Cameroon
Canada
Colombia
Cyprus (4)
Czech Republic
Denmark
Duba
Ethiopia
France (7)

Gambia
Germany
Gibraltar (4)
Guatemala
Honduras
Hungary
India (7)
Indonesia (3)
Italy (2
Jamaica (2)
Kenya (3)
Lesotho (3)
Malawi (4)
Malaysia
Mauritius (3)
Namibia (9)
Netherlands (2)
Nigeria (3)
Norway (2)
Oman (2)
Pakistan

Panama
Paraguay
Philippines (4)
Romania
Saudi Arabia (3)
Sierra Leone (3)
Singapore (6)
Slovakia
South Africa (4)
Sri Lanka
St Helena (3)
St Kitts–Nevis
St Lucia Nevis
Swaziland
Sweden
Thailand
Tonga
Tristan Da Cunha
Uganda (7)
United Arab Emirates
Zimbabwe (3)

(*Source: Hansard*, 22 November 1995)

Countries which sent police personnel to the UK to study crowd control techniques between 1981 and 1989:

Australia
Belgium
Botswana
Brazil
Canada
France
Germany

Guyana
Hong Kong
Japan
Kuwait
Mexico
Netherlands
New Zealand

Pakistan
Sri Lanka
Tunisia
Turkey
United Arab Emirates
Uruguay

(*Source: Hansard*, 2 February 1990)

APPENDIX III

Further Reading

The Amnesty International Annual Report 1995 and 1996, Amnesty International

China: No One is Safe, Amnesty International, Amnesty International, 1996

China: Persistent Human Rights Violations in Tibet, Amnesty International 1995

East Timor: 20 Years of Violations, Amnesty International 1995

Indonesia and East Timor: Power and Impunity – Human Rights Under the New Order, Amnesty International, 1994

Malawi: Prison Conditions, Cruel Punishments and Detention Without Trial, Amnesty International, 1992

Mozambique: The Role of the United Nations in the Protection of Human Rights under the General Peace Agreement, Amnesty International, 1993

Pakistan: The Pattern Persists: Torture, deaths in custody, extrajudicial executions and disappearances' under the PPP Government, Amnesty International, 1995

Rwanda: Arming the Perpetrators of the Genocide, Amnesty International, 1995

Sierra Leone: Human Rights Abuses in a War Against Civilians, Amnesty International, 1995

Turkey: A Policy of Denial, Amnesty International, 1995

Turkey: A Time for Action, Amnesty International, 1994

United States of America: Human Rights Violations – A Summary of Amnesty International's Concerns, Amnesty International, 1995

A European Code of Conduct on the Arms Trade, Saferworld, *British American Security Information Council* – World Development Movement, 1995

Gunrunners' Gold, World Development Movement, 1995

The Military Balance 1994-5, The International Institute for Strategic Studies, Brassey's 1994

Stockholm International Peace Research Institute Yearbook, Oxford University Press, 1995

Truth is a Difficult Concept: Inside the Scott Inquiry, Richard Norton-Taylor, Fourth Estate Ltd, 1995

To buy Amnesty International reports listed here, or for details of other Amnesty International reports, contact the Information Office at

Amnesty International UK,
99-119 Rosebery Avenue,
London EC1R 4RE
Telephone 0171 814 6200